The Little Manual of
MEDITATION

By the same author

- The Little Manual of Success
- The Little Manual of Enlightenment
- The Little Manual of Happiness

The Little Manual of MEDITATION

15 Effective Ways to Discover Your Inner Self

SoulWords
Vikas Malkani
Best-selling author of
THE LITTLE MANUAL OF ENLIGHTENMENT

UNICORN BOOKS

This edition published by :
UNICORN BOOKS (P) Ltd., New Delhi-110002
F-2/16 , Ansari Road, Daryaganj, New Delhi-110002
☎ 23275434, 23262683, 23262783 • *Fax:* 011-23257790
E-mail: unicornbooks@vsnl.com
Website: www.unicornbooks.in • www.kidscorner.in

Distributors
Pustak Mahal, Delhi
E-mail: info@pustakmahal.com • *Website:* www.pustakmahal.com

Year of Publication : 2008
Edition: 2010

ISBN: 978-81-7806-142-9

Editorial and design: Write Media

Original Edition Published by: SoulWords Publishing Pte Ltd., Singapore
www.soulwordspublishing.com

Meditation is not a means to an end.
It is both the means and the end.

J. Krishnamurti

To my beloved master, Swami Rama of the Himalayas,
who through meditation introduced me to my Self.
I am eternally grateful and indebted to you!

Meditation has been the grounding force in my life;
it has kept me stable regardless of the externals.
Meditation has shown me the truth of my own existence.
It is a treasure that cannot ever be taken away from me.

Testimonials for Vikas Malkani and His Teachings

I have become more aware, more focussed and am more mindful of my interaction with others. Meditation has given me easy and quick techniques to get into this state as and when I want.

Sue Olivier, South Africa

Meditation has shown me the path to living in the moment. I am definitely calmer and can see each day fully. I feel a sense of lightness within myself.

Rhonda Howarth-Kuo, Australia

It has made me more conscious of the many blessings in my life. It has given me calmness and I live consciously every second of every day.

Kit, Singapore

Meditation has made me calmer and happier. It has given me a completely new perspective on life and I now interact with the world very differently. Definitely a technique I would recommend to others.

Sudhanshu Sarronwala, India

Meditation has and is continuing to help clear clutter from my mind—all the 'non-value' adding stuff such as unnecessary worries, unfounded suspicions and fears. It has given me clarity, focus and energy to deal with work and relationships. I have been meditating for over two years now with great benefits.

Ruth Chua, Founder,
Gaia Yoga, Singapore

Meditation is one tool that helps me in my daily life to become calmer, less irritated by unimportant things. It gives me the opportunity to explore myself, being together with no one else but myself, quieting my restless mind. But the most beautiful thing is that meditation brings you in contact with your real, true Self. This morning while meditating, I was able to catch a glimpse of my soul, realising what beautiful beings we are—pure light, love and without any limits. I felt what it means to love unconditionally and to be free of fear and restrictions. It was one of the most wonderful experiences of my life, hard to describe, mind blowing, divine and utterly peaceful. I am very thankful for this experience and I am deeply grateful for the guidance of my teacher Vikas Malkani.

Antoinette (Toni) Biehlmeier, holistic therapist, Germany

Meditation has made me realise that I create my own experience of life. I am much more confident now, relaxed and more optimistic.

Lweendo Gravelle

Meditation has shown me that I have full control over my life. It gives me a greater ability to see things with clarity. I have become much more appreciative of the blessings of my life.

Janis Tan, Singapore

Meditation has benefited me tremendously as it allows me to be more objective in my life, seeing all sides of it and choosing my action. It helps me to relax my body and calm my mind. Meditation makes me feel in control and centred.

Jarrod Benson, UK

Contents

Author's Note

In every culture and society, all over the world, people are educated in the skills needed to function in that culture—how to talk, think, work and investigate the objects and experiences of the external world. When in school and college we learn sciences such as biology, ecology and chemistry in order to understand the world we live in, but no one really teaches us how to understand or attend to our inner dimensions.

We merely learn to assimilate the goals, fashions and values of our society, without knowing ourselves. This leaves us ignorant about our true nature and dependent on the advice and suggestions of others. In this book, my attempt is to explain the importance of learning meditation. For meditation is very different to all the things we learn in our formal education. It is very essential, too.

Meditation is a subtle and precise approach. It is a simple technique of learning to pay attention to and understanding the various levels of ourselves—the body, the breathing process, the aspects of stress and so on.

As time progresses, you may find that you like the positive results from meditation. The act of meditation brings with it increased joyfulness, clarity and awareness. It also helps you to enjoy the relief of the physical, nervous and mental symptoms of stress.

I am certain that *The Little Manual of Meditation* will guide you to locate your inner self—the real you.

Vikas Malkani

| Chapter One |

Pay Attention

Meditation is a kind of medicine—its use is only for the time being. Once you have learned the quality, then you need not do any particular meditation; then the meditation has to spread all over your life.

Osho

Meditation implies a sense of 'attending to' or 'paying attention to' something. While meditating, you pay attention to those dimensions of yourself that are not observed or known—that is, your own inner levels, lying deep within you. These deeper levels are more profound than the process of thinking, analysing, daydreaming or experiencing emotions or memories. These are the levels of awareness that help you to relate to your own self and bring you in harmony with your being.

Meditation involves a type of inner attention that is quiet, concentrated and, at the same time, relaxed. There is nothing strenuous or difficult about creating this inner attention. In fact, meditation is a process that is restful and relaxing for the mind.

In the beginning, the greatest difficulty is that the mind has not been trained to create this inner attention. With training and practise this focussing is accomplished. When that happens, the rest flows. It is almost like a gentle river, flowing with ease towards its source.

It is very easy to begin the practice of meditation. It actually all starts in the mind. You simply have to *decide* that you are going to take up meditation. Once you do that, you will find that you do not have to do anything different or demanding physically than what you have already been used to. Your lifestyle will not change, but your life will! Take my word for it. Meditation brings with it a certain mindfulness that cannot be described in words. It can only be experienced.

Your meditation will not require you to adopt any strange or foreign habits, neither will you have to meditate for long or extended periods of time in order to progress and observe the benefits. All you have to do is to be with the moment and enjoy the practice of meditation. Your body will become more creative and focussed and you will also notice significant improvements in your health and relationships.

Be Alert

Just as there are many different paths you can take to climb a mountain, there are a variety of seemingly 'different' meditation techniques that you can follow. Yet, all have the same goal—achieving a state of inner concentration, calmness and serenity. Any method that helps you to achieve this is beneficial. Many valid techniques exist, so there is really no difference between one type of authentic meditation and

★ Meditation involves a type of inner attention that is quiet, concentrated and, at the same time, relaxed ★

another, as long as they help you to be more attentive and to focus on your inner self.

Being alert and mindful is the first step in the practice of meditation. Initially you would have to make a determined effort to decide and to begin meditating. You will require as much determination thereafter to stay on the meditative path and to come back to it with regularity.

It is only when you have made this a part of your daily routine that you would have truly taken your first steps in transforming yourself into a focussed individual, at peace with yourself.

The important thing, therefore, is your decision to practise meditation. With that decision in place, the mind will gradually focus on actions that will then seem to follow naturally. Flow with this tide of thought and action and soon you will be meditating and reaching into your inner self—or that part of your being that has so far been untouched.

As Osho, the Indian spiritual Master, observed, "Remember one thing: meditation means awareness. Whatsoever you do with awareness is meditation. Action is not the question, but the quality that you bring to your action. Walking can be a meditation if you walk alertly. Sitting can be a meditation if you sit alertly. Listening to the birds can be a meditation if you listen with awareness. Just listening to the inner noise of your mind can be a meditation if you remain alert and watchful."

Osho also believes that even an action such as taking a bath is a spiritual exercise. Focus on the water as it falls on your body; realise that this is the water that makes up a large part of you. Become one with it.

★ Being alert and mindful is the first step in the practice of meditation ★

Try bringing this attention to all that you do over the day. If you are reading, be with the words. If you are working, concentrate on the job at hand. These are all acts of meditation, though you may not think so at first. Believe me, paying attention to all that you do, every single act, is the most powerful form of meditation. It brings you closer to your self and to the activity. In these spaces between the thought and the action, you find yourself and your Creator.

Way 1

Decide!

Meditation always proves to be restful and relaxing

| Chapter Two |

Look Within

Meditation is the tongue of the soul and the language of our spirit.

Jeremy Taylor

When we observe life carefully, we realise that right from our childhood we have only been trained in how to examine and verify things in the external world and that no one has actually taught us how to look within. In a sense, the human being remains a stranger to himself or herself. With a lack of training we are not able to reach within or have a better understanding of our deeper selves.

Often, therefore, while trying to establish various sorts of relationships in the external world, we are not able to connect our real selves to the outside world. That is why few of these relationships really seem to work. Success eludes us; confusion and disappointment prevails. We find that we are unable to communicate meaningfully with the world around us.

Very little of the mind is cultivated by our formal educational system. We are often taught only to interact with the external realities. That part of the mind that dreams and sleeps, the vast realm of the unconscious, which is the reservoir of all our experiences and emotions, remains unknown and undisciplined; it is not subjected to any control or direction.

There are no teachers to guide this aspect of our persona. We are always taught how to move and behave in the external world, but we are never really taught how to be still and examine what is within ourselves.

This journey into the inner self is actually the pathway to all our external relations becoming enriched and even joyful

When you learn to sit still, you attain a kind of joy that can only be experienced by a human being through meditation. All the other joys in the world are transient and momentary, but the joy of meditation is immense and everlasting. This is not an exaggeration but a simple fact, a truth that is supported by the great sages—those who renounced the world and attained the truth and those who attained the truth without renouncing the world.

"Meditation is seeing God in you," believes the Indian spiritual guru, Sri Sri Ravi Shankar. And where does this God reside? In your deep inner recesses—some call it the soul, some the spirit. In *The Little Manual of Enlightenment*, I have dwelt on this topic in greater detail. This journey into the inner self is actually the pathway to all our external relations becoming enriched and even joyful. Meditation is a powerful tool that, in fact, helps us in connecting with our external world. Just try it. You will find yourself exploring new vistas. By relating to your inner self you will be able to connect with the world around you more easily.

The Wandering Mind

Our mind has a tendency to wander into the grooves of its old patterns and then it imagines those experiences in the future as well. The mind does not really know how to be in the present, here and now. Only meditation teaches us to fully experience the now, which is a part of the eternal.

In meditation, the journey is of utmost importance. As Alan Watts wrote, "We could say that meditation doesn't have a reason or doesn't have a purpose. In this respect it's unlike almost all other things we do except perhaps making music and dancing. When we make music we don't do it in order to reach a certain point, such as the end of the composition. If that were the purpose of music then obviously the fastest players would be the best.

"Also, when we are dancing we are not aiming to arrive at a particular place on the floor as in a journey. When we dance, the journey itself is the point, as when we play music the playing itself is the point. And exactly the same thing is true in meditation. Meditation is the discovery that the point of life is always arrived at in the immediate moment."

When, with the help of meditative techniques, the mind is focussed at a point, it attains the power of penetrating into the deeper levels of one's being. Then, the mind does not create any distraction or deviations; it fully attains the power of concentration, which is a prerequisite for meditation.

Gradually, over a period of time, the mind is comforted by this focus and near stillness that it acquires. This is an important discipline in the journey that leads us to a meditative understanding.

Experience Progress

To begin this path, understand clearly what meditation is. Select a practice that is comfortable for you and do it consistently and regularly for some time, every day. It is best if you do it at the same time each day, if possible.

★ Only meditation teaches us to fully experience the now, which is a part of the eternal ★

Our bodies respond best when we regulate them and follow a routine. That is why when we are babies we usually sleep at a fixed time, wake up at a set time and eat at a regular time. As we grow up we generally abandon routine. We are influenced by the impulses of only our external interactions and relationships and tend to lose the value that routine gave us in our childhood. This important place that routine played in our lives needs to be reclaimed. We need to remind ourselves about the importance of routine and return to it consciously.

Do Not Lose Patience

In the modern world, students often become impatient easily and they tend to practise meditation only for brief periods and soon give up on it. They conclude that there is no value or authenticity in the technique. This is like a child who plants a tulip bulb and is frustrated because s/he sees no flowers in a week!

You will definitely experience progress if you meditate regularly. At first, you may see the progress in terms of immediate physical relaxation and calmness. Later, you may notice other, more subtle benefits.

Some of the most important benefits of meditation make themselves known gradually over a period of time, and are not dramatic or easily observed. Persist in your meditation and you will observe progress.

Before you begin to meditate, you should have some faith in the process by which meditation helps you to look within.

In order to meditate, you will need to learn:

- How to relax the body.
- How to sit in a comfortable, steady position.
- How to make your breathing process serene. Remember, breathing and meditation have strong links.
- How to witness the objects travelling in the terrain of your mind.

- How to inspect the quality of thoughts and learn to promote or strengthen those that are positive and helpful in your growth.

★ You will definitely experience progress if you meditate regularly ★

- How to prevent yourself from being disturbed in any situation, whether you judge it as being good or bad.

The meditative state is the highest state of existence. If you meditate with a clear understanding of what it is, and with the appropriate techniques and attitudes, you will find it refreshing and energising. If you learn how to look within, you will certainly find that the outside world will resonate in harmony with you and your thoughts.

Way 2

Sit still

Meditation gives you a positive outlook

|Chapter Three|

Make an Investment

When we raise ourselves through meditation to what unites us with the spirit, we quicken something within us that is eternal and unlimited by birth and death.

Rudolf Steiner

Meditation is the best time investment you can make. If you believe that health is wealth, then the time you set aside every day for your meditation session will make you a prosperous person. This is the kind of wealth that will enrich you in body, mind and spirit.

We find time to do many things during our waking hours. If you were to do an audit of what was necessary and what was useful to you and list all that was not either, you would find that the time for meditation is actually quite easily available to you. So, to begin with, remove from your mind this self-created mental barrier of lack of time. Try telling yourself, "I will find the time," and believe the many who have passed this way that you *will* find the time.

Unlike rituals that often specify time, space and duration, meditation gives the freedom, even to beginners, to decide for how long and where and how many times in a day you will meditate. The practice will grow on you and the peace and balance that you achieve even in a short time will spur you on to do more.

Heal Yourself

Many studies have aptly shown that meditation significantly improves our health levels. The stress released and the energy produced when we meditate activate the body's own healing forces.

★ Remove from your mind this self-created mental barrier of lack of time ★

All healing comes from within. Often drugs do nothing to remove the cause of the problems; they merely suppress the symptoms in a seeming cure. In fact, in most cases, drugs produce many harmful side effects, thereby aggravating the situation. Meditation is an excellent complement to conventional medicine or surgery. Patients who meditate heal themselves faster.

Get Yourself a Good Rest

Theoretically, we should wake up every morning feeling fresh and alive, ready to tackle whatever the day has in store for us. But this is not the case always. The problem is that we do not always sleep peacefully, or long enough.

Physical discomfort, mental worries or just not feeling relaxed are obstacles to a good sleep that can lead to rest and relaxation. This is where meditation comes to the rescue. By giving our nervous system an additional period of deep rest twice a day, we can compensate for a bad night's sleep, so that we feel good and have a productive day. Try to keep gaps in your day for even five minutes of meditation. Studies show that during both sleep and meditation, our metabolic rate slows down. The metabolic rate refers to how quickly the body uses oxygen to burn up the nutrients from the food we consume to produce energy. A low metabolic rate indicates that the body is not using up much oxygen and is in a more restful state. The metabolic rate is considered a good indicator of how relaxed the body is.

The remarkable thing is that meditation produces a lower metabolic rate than sleep. During sleep, it takes four or five hours to produce an eight per cent drop in metabolic rate, while during a thirty-minute meditation, we achieve a drop between ten per cent and twenty per cent. This means meditation produces a much deeper state of rest than sleep and in a much shorter time.

In addition, alpha waves are produced by the brain during meditation, which also signifies a deep state of rest. Alpha waves are not usually produced during sleep. However, this does not mean that you do not need to sleep, for sleep has many other functions besides producing rest and overall mental balance.

Rejuvenate Yourself

When you rest the nervous system by meditation, your brain works at peak efficiency. This means you will display more intelligence, more creativity and more feelings. This is especially significant as happiness and success depend, to a large extent, on these three factors. Deep rest also makes you feel good since it relaxes the nervous system and allows it to be recharged with energy. The deep rest produced by meditation is mainly due to the reduction in thought when you meditate.

★ The remarkable thing is that meditation produces a lower metabolic rate than sleep ★

Meditation Calms the Brain

Thoughts actually produce waves that are registered in the brain as electrical activity. If our thoughts are excessive (as they are in most of us), then this electrical activity becomes excessive and it is a disturbance to the brain. We feel this unpleasantness and tension in the mind and call it stress.

Meditation greatly reduces the amount of electrical activity in the brain. The brain becomes calm and we can feel this in the mind as a pleasant peacefulness. In meditation the brain is given a rest, which allows it to recuperate and rejuvenate.

Deep rest also activates the body's healing processes, allowing rejuvenation of the body to occur. Once the metabolic rate slows down, the body directs some of its energy for healing and rejuvenation. We become much healthier as a result of regular meditation. Minor, sometimes major, health disorders disappear and we start to look and feel younger.

Disease is actually a very apt word, for it implies not being at ease (dis-ease).

Not only the body, but the mind also feels rejuvenated. For probably the first time in your life, your mind, through meditation, gets a rest during the day in addition to the night. The body and the mind have in-built abilities to recharge, they just need the right conditions. Meditation provides you the key to both of these.

Therefore, to reiterate, meditation actually leads to rejuvenation because meditation promises a deeper rest than sleep, in a much shorter time. This causes our brain to work at peak efficiency: we show more intelligence, creativity and feeling. It also makes us feel good, since deep rest relaxes the nervous system and recharges it with energy. Deep rest reactivates the body's healing forces, allowing rejuvenation of the body and mind to occur.

Here are some tips to make your meditation more effective:

- It is possible to meditate at any time, but an ideal time is at sunrise.

- Practise is absolutely necessary. It promotes your inner worth to practise regularly and at least once, ideally twice a day, in the morning and evening. I feel that even five minutes works well for me.

- Quiet surroundings are obviously helpful to the meditative process. Outer harmony, such as that found in a beautiful park or at a picturesque lake, furthers your inner balance. At home, it is helpful to create a special place for meditation. Ask your family to cooperate with you by not disturbing you when you are meditating.

- Prepare for your meditation session by first washing your hands and face and generally freshening up. This dispels drowsiness and promotes a wakeful, energetic disposition.

★ Deep rest reactivates the body's healing forces, allowing rejuvenation of the body and mind to occur ★

- It is good to sit with the spine straight, whether it is on a chair or on the floor in the lotus posture.

- Begin by taking a few deep breaths, expelling all tension in the body and concerns of the mind.

- Consciously relax your entire body, especially the chest and the facial muscles.

- Resolve to dedicate yourself to the meditation process wholeheartedly.

- Tell yourself, mentally or aloud, that, for the duration of the meditation, nothing else matters.

- Be willing to surrender yourself and encounter the greater self.

- Now begin your meditation, whatever your technique may be: the practice of mindfulness, mantra recitation, contemplation of a particularly meaningful image or abstract concentration.

- Do not be concerned about distracting thoughts, sensations or emotions—neither welcome nor repress them. Simply let them be and persist in your practice. Sooner or later your inner world will become calm.

- Remember, there are no good or bad meditation sessions. All that really matters is that you seriously engage in the meditative process, regardless of the content that arises. Every meditation is a step towards greater inner freedom.

- Do not abandon your meditation at the first impulse to do so, especially when the going is rough. Stick with it for a while. Try to sit for at least fifteen minutes at the beginning and, after a few weeks of practise, for at least half-an-hour. Often you can overcome the initial resistance and then you may find yourself in a completely different inner space. You will learn to recognise that there is a natural ending to every meditation, where it seems appropriate to get up.

- After your meditation is over, review the session and affirm its positive aspects.

- Throughout the day, try to recall the inner peace created by deep meditation.

★ All that matters is that you seriously engage in the meditative process ★

- Take on the discipline of not chatting about your meditation experiences to everyone because inner experiences must be shared with all honesty and truth with your spiritual teacher only. Talking to others would merely dissipate your energy and strengthen your ego.

Find a technique of meditation that you are comfortable with and make it a part of your life. It will be the wisest investment that you will make.

Way 3

Relax!

Meditation expels all tension from the body

| Chapter Four |

Improve Your Health

Meditation does what nothing else can do. It introduces you to your Self.

Swami Rama

Meditation is therapeutic from the moment you decide to take it up seriously. It helps to relax the tension of the gross and subtle muscles and the autonomous nervous system. It provides freedom from mental stress. A person in meditation attains a tranquil mind and this helps the body's immune system by limiting its reaction to stress and strain.

You will find that even a few days of sincere effort will help you to control your appetite and severe reactions, such as anger, to a certain degree. Meditation will also decrease the need for sleep and energise the body and mind. Writers, poets and thinkers often express interest in the process of becoming creative and using their intuition—the finest and most evolved of all aspects of knowledge. Meditation is a systematic way of using this aspect of human brilliance in our daily life.

Our health is greatly influenced by meditation. In today's world, most diseases can be classified to some degree as psychosomatic, having their origins in, or being influenced by, the human mind, thoughts and emotions. Scientists have begun to recognise that these diseases cannot be cured only by the conventional methods of orthodox medicine or psychotherapy, because if the disease originates in the mind or is caused by various emotional reactions, how is it possible for external therapy alone to restore your health?

If you rely only on external remedies and do not seek to understand your own mind and emotions, you may merely become dependent on a therapist or a physician for help. In contrast, the process of meditation makes you self-reliant and helps you attain the inner strength necessary to deal more effectively with all your problems, including those related to your health.

You have to start the meditation process yourself. No one is going to make you do this

Remember the key words here are 'seek to'. You have to start the meditation process yourself. No one is going to make you do this.

Learn to Relax

You know that you have made a good decision by opting for meditation when you realise the stress released as a result of it. You learn to relax and that is a great feeling. It is a feeling that you deserve and, somewhere along the line, you have forgotten to sense it. When you do begin to recognise it, enjoy it to the maximum, for this is what you deserve. And, once you do that, let life take over again. You will see that a higher power has taken control. All you have to do is surrender to it.

Regrets and grudges, worries and anxious moments, will keep coming along. What you have to remember is that you can control all these at will—you can decide when you want to tackle your problems, what you want to ignore and when you want to relax. It is the habit of restful awareness and it can be done easiest through meditation, the ultimate health management programme. You will learn to let go of the past and live in the present moment totally. Other very important health benefits are:

Benefit 1: *Reduction of blood pressure*

In an American study on stress management, thirty-five people with an average systolic blood pressure of one-hundred-and-forty-six were placed under observation. After just a few weeks of meditation, their blood pressure came down from the borderline high range to the normal range.

This is far better than taking drugs, which have side effects and do nothing to tackle the cause of the problem. Addressing only the effect of the problem and not the cause is never a long-term solution.

Benefit 2: *Improved sleep*

When we meditate regularly, we tend to fall asleep quicker and our sleep is deeper. This means we get more and better quality sleep. As a result, we wake up feeling more fresh and alive than before. We also feel more energetic and calm throughout the day.

Benefit 3: ***Increased circulation to all organs and glands***

Relaxed blood vessels allow increased blood flow to all parts of the body. Increased blood flow to the brain means we feel fresher and can think more clearly. It also helps us to prevent strokes. Increased blood flow to the digestive system means it will function better and we will digest and assimilate food better.

★ Meditation is the ultimate health management programme ★

Benefit 4: ***Balancing of the two hemispheres of the brain***

Studies show that meditation has a balancing and harmonising effect on the right and left hemispheres of the brain. Our left hemisphere is responsible for thinking. It is the logical, analytical side of the brain. The right side is responsible for our emotions.

Owing to the pace of modern life, many of us tend to operate more from the left hemisphere. We think too much and analyse too much at the expense of our feelings. Meditation allows us to have the correct balance of logical, analytical thought and emotions.

Benefit 5: ***Controlling asthma***

A clinical research conducted by Ron Honsberger and Archie F. Wilson in the USA reported that asthmatic patients showed improvements in their asthma after meditation. Ninety-four per cent of the group showed less air passage resistance, fifty-five per cent showed improvements as reported by their personal physicians and seventy-five per cent stated that they themselves felt an improvement.

Benefit 6: *Reduction of mental tension*

Up to seventy per cent of all health problems are said to be psychosomatic. So it is easy to understand how a reduction in stress due to meditation can help cure many of these disorders. In a study carried out by Dr A. Kasamatsu and Dr Hirai of the University of Tokyo, it was found that when Zen monks meditated, they produced a predominance of alpha waves. In addition, the alpha waves increased in amplitude and regularity during meditation. Similar results were found by researchers in India when they conducted studies on yogis during meditation.

Benefit 7: *Keeping you young*

Meditation stimulates your glands. Hormone levels in those who meditate are similar to those in people up to ten years younger. This is one of the reasons why meditators look and feel young. At the same time, meditation causes a reduction in the production of your stress hormones—adrenaline and nor-adrenaline.

Benefit 8: *Reversal of ageing*

Biomechanical age measures how old a person is physiologically. According to a study conducted in the USA, as a group, long-term meditators who have been practising meditation for more than five years were physiologically twelve years younger than their chronological age, as measured by reduction of blood pressure and better near-point vision and auditory discrimination. Short-term meditators were physiologically five years younger than their chronological age. The study took into consideration the effects of diet and exercise.

Benefit 9: *Increased alertness*

In their electroencephalographic (EEG) studies, a French team comprising Jean-Paul Banquet and Maurice Sailhan reported that, during meditation, a greater proportion of alpha waves were produced compared to delta waves. This indicates a heightened level of wakefulness. In addition, the ratio of beta waves to alpha waves was reduced, indicating a more relaxed state. It is this unique combination of deep relaxation and increased alertness that differentiates meditation from other relaxation techniques and sleep. It is referred to as the meditative state of consciousness or the super-conscious state and indicates the emergence of the higher consciousness.

★ Hormone levels in meditators are similar to those in people up to ten years younger ★

Benefit 10: *Optimises brain function*

Reports published in the *International Journal of Neuroscience* claim that higher levels of EEG coherence, measured during the practise of meditation, are significantly correlated with an increased fluency of verbal IQ, decreased neuroticism, more clear experiences of transcendental consciousness and increased neurological efficiency.

Benefit 11: *Decreases the dependency on drugs*

A study on the effect of meditation on drug use was undertaken in the USA by Dr R.K. Wallace, Dr H. Benson and associates. Two questionnaires were initially sent to almost two thousand people who were all experienced meditators. About eighteen hundred people responded. The subjects were asked to carefully record their drug-use habit before and after starting meditation. In the six-month period prior to starting meditation, seventy-eight per cent had used either marijuana and hashish or both, and twenty-eight per cent were heavy users (once a day or more).

After six months of regular meditation, only thirty-seven per cent continued to use marijuana—that is, a forty per cent drop. After twenty-one months of meditation, only twelve per cent continued to use marijuana—that is, again a forty per cent drop. After twenty-one months of meditation, only twelve per cent continue to use marijuana—a sixty-six per cent drop. Of those who still took drugs, only one was a heavy user.

Meditation was even more successful with LSD users. After twenty-two months of meditation, ninety-seven per cent of LSD users had given it up. There was also a high rate of success with heavy narcotics including heroin, opium, morphine and cocaine. Before meditation, seventeen per cent used these drugs and after a twenty-two- to twenty-three-month period of meditation, only one per cent continued to use them.

★ Meditation helps us to live life the way it was always meant to be ★

Now, when questioned why the meditators gave up drugs, the general response was that they enjoyed the profound feelings from meditation more than the feelings aroused by drugs.

Anyone can take up meditation. It is a simple, natural and effortless technique to still the mind and make us experience peace and tranquillity, leading us to our true inner selves. It also helps us to live life the way it was always meant to be, a life full of love, laughter, freedom and good health.

Way 4

Be strong

Meditation makes you self-reliant
and helps you attain inner strength

| Chapter Five |

Correct Your Posture

I discovered the secret of the sea in meditation upon the dew drop.

Kahlil Gibran

Meditation is like a package deal. You have to want to try it, you have to find the right time for it, you have to learn a technique that suits your style and, along with that, you have to learn the right postures. In return you become more focussed, improve your health, get better sleep, more energy and also reduce your frustrations. Meditation is a simple technique that almost everyone can enjoy. So get into the right posture and start.

In modern living the right posture is one of the lesser understood phenomena. In fact, whether for breathing exercises or for yogic asanas, the posture is the most crucial element. This deserves close attention. Often our posture has been so neglected by us that its correction is the first prerequisite for our body. This will enable us to concentrate on those aspects of contemplation, meditation and yoga that will help us attain harmony with our physical environment.

Be mindful, then, of the need for maintaining a correct posture. At an early stage get all the help you can towards this. The benefits are many.

Sit Straight

★ Meditation is a simple technique that almost everyone can enjoy ★

For a good meditation posture you need to be still, steady, relaxed and comfortable. Now make the breathing process serene and then allow your mind to become quiet and focussed. If the body moves, sways, twitches or aches, it will distract you from meditation. Some people have the misconception that to meditate, you must sit in a complicated, cross-legged position called the 'lotus pose'. Fortunately, this is not true. There is actually only one important prerequisite for a good meditation posture, and that is, it must allow you to keep the head, neck and trunk of the body aligned so that you can breathe freely and diaphragmatically.

Centre the Head, Neck and Trunk

In all the meditative postures, the head and neck should be centred, so that the neck is not twisted or turned to either side, nor is the head held too forward. The head should be supported by the neck and held directly over the shoulders without creating any tension in the neck or shoulders. Keep your face forward, with your eyes gently closed. Simply allow the eyes to close and do not create any pressure on them.

Some people have been told to try to force their gaze upwards to a specific point in their forehead. This position creates strain and tension in the eyes and may even lead to a headache. There are some yogic positions that involve specific gazes, but they are not used during meditation. Just let all the facial muscles relax. The mouth should also be gently closed, without any tension in the jaw. All breathing is done through the nostrils.

Relax the Shoulders, Arms and Hands

In all the meditative positions, your shoulders and arms are relaxed and allowed to rest gently on the knees. Your arms should be so completely relaxed, that if someone were to pick up your hand, your arm would be limp. You can gently join the thumb and index fingers in a position called the 'finger lock'. This mudra or gesture creates a circle, which you may think of, symbolically, as a small circuit that recycles energy within, rather than extending your energy outward.

Be Comfortable

There are many positions that allow you to sit comfortably, keeping the spine aligned, without twisting your legs or creating any discomfort. In fact, the arms and legs are not really important in meditation. What is important is that the spine be correctly aligned.

Here are some easy positions that you can follow:

Position 1: Maitriasana *or friendship pose*

In *maitriasana*, you sit comfortably on a chair or a bench, with your feet flat on the floor and your hands resting on your lap. *Maitriasana* can be used by anyone, even those who are not very flexible or comfortable sitting on the floor. This posture allows you to begin the process of meditation without creating any difficulties for the body.

Position 2: Sukhasana *or easy pose*

If you are somewhat more flexible, you may want to begin sitting in an alternative position, called the *sukhasana* or 'easy pose'. For this, you sit in a simple, cross-legged position on the floor or a platform.

★ What is important is that the spine be correctly aligned during meditation ★

In 'easy pose', the feet are placed on the floor under the opposite knees, and each knee rests gently on the opposite foot. Place a folded blanket underneath yourself, so that your knees or ankles do not receive too much pressure. Your meditation seat should be firm, but neither too hard nor shaky. The seat should not be so high that it disturbs your body position.

If your legs are less flexible or your thigh muscles are tight, you may find that your knees remain fairly off the floor. Several warm-up stretching postures will be beneficial in developing greater flexibility, thereby increasing your comfort.

Whatever position you select, use it regularly and avoid frequent attempts at new postures—if you work regularly on one sitting posture, it will become comfortable and steady over a period of time.

Position 3: Swastikasana *or auspicious pose*

The 'auspicious pose' offers several advantages to those who can sit in this posture comfortably. If your legs are fairly flexible, you may actually find it more comfortable than the 'easy pose', especially for longer periods of meditation. Since the position has a wider foundation, it distributes the body weight more directly on the floor and is somewhat steadier and less likely to lead to swaying or other bodily movements.

In *swastikasana*, the knees rest directly on the floor, rather than on the feet. One advantage of this posture, for some students, is that the ankle receives less weight or pressure.

To develop the 'auspicious pose' you can begin by sitting comfortably in your meditation seat. Bend the left leg at the knee and place the left foot alongside the right thigh. The sole or the bottom of the left foot may be flat against the inside of the right thigh. Next, the right knee is bent and the right foot is placed gently on the left calf, with the bottom of the foot against the thigh. The upper surface of the right foot is gently placed between the thigh and the back of the left calf, tucking in the toes. Finally, with your hand, you gently bring the toes of your left foot up between the right thigh and calf, so that the big toe is now visible. This creates a symmetrical and stable posture, which is very effective for meditation. Even though the above description may sound complicated, you will find that if you follow the directions, it is not difficult.

For beginners, the 'auspicious pose' may not be comfortable initially because they lack flexibility in their legs. You can certainly sit in any individual variation of a cross-legged pose that allows you to be steady and keep the body still without jerkiness or swaying, or you may begin with the *maitriasana*. The point to be noted is that it is more important to keep the head, neck and trunk correctly positioned, so that the spine is aligned, than to put your legs in some particular position.

★ Whatever position you select, use it regularly and avoid frequent attempts at new postures ★

Do Not Slump

People these days tend to have a poor posture because of the bad habits that they have developed by the lack of walking and by sitting in front of the computer. Owing to this, the muscles that are meant to support the spinal column remain underdeveloped and the spine tends to curve with age, distorting the body. When you first begin sitting in meditation, you may notice that your back muscles are weak and that after a few minutes of sitting, you tend to slump forward.

Actually, this problem can be solved in a very short while if you begin to pay attention to your posture throughout the day while sitting, standing and walking. Adjust your posture whenever you notice that you are slumping. In this way, the back muscles will begin to do their job appropriately.

Some students with poor postures ask if they can do their meditation leaning back against a wall for support. In the beginning, you can do this to develop a correctly aligned posture or to check your alignment, although it is not good to remain dependent on such support.

It is best to work consciously and attentively with your posture from the very start. Ask a friend to check, or examine your posture while watching sideways in a mirror. If the spinal column is correctly aligned, you will not feel the knobs of the spinal vertebrae jutting out while you run your hand up your back.

Be Kind to Your Body

Most people find it easier to sit on the floor if they use a folded blanket. This provides a good padding for the entire area. You can also use a thick cushion or pillow under the buttocks and hips for supporting that part of the body, which is three to four inches off the floor. This will also keep your spine correctly aligned. Elevating the buttocks in this manner seems to relieve much of the pressure on the hip joints and the knees.

You will be amazed to see the difference it makes.

As you become more flexible and comfortable, you may find that you can use a thinner cushion and eventually sit flat on the floor. However, it is important to keep the spine aligned and not allow it to curve over, disturbing your posture. Be patient in developing your sitting posture; you will find that your body gradually becomes more flexible and that you can sit for longer periods much more comfortably.

★ From the beginning, it is best to work consciously and attentively with your posture ★

If you have made up your mind about giving meditation a try, then all you need is determination. Set aside just fifteen to twenty minutes every other day to begin with. But there is one rule, when thinking about starting to meditate, you have to *want to* succeed.

Seat yourself in the correct way and get ready to meditate. You will be amazed at the immense relaxation it will give to both, your body and your mind.

Way 5

Be patient

Meditation is a simple technique that almost everyone can enjoy

| Chapter Six |

Breathe Right

When the breath wanders the mind also is unsteady. But when the breath is calmed the mind, too, will be still, and the yogi achieves long life.

Svatmarama

Breathing exercises, which are used in all types of meditation as an essential preparation, are extremely relaxing for the nervous system. There are many such exercises that you can follow in order to get the maximum flow of oxygen into your body. Remember, if you want results, you need to do these continuously and on a permanent basis.

The best time to do these exercises is in the morning. That is the time when you are fresh and your nerve centres are alert. Your body has had a good night's rest and it is ready to be used. Your mind, too, is much sharper in the morning. You are able to think clearly and the body is sending out all the right signals.

The following exercises are very important for beginners:

Exercise 1: *The complete breath*

The complete breath helps expand the capacity of the lungs and is excellent as a physical and mental energising exercise. If possible, do this exercise in front of an open window or, even better, go outdoors.

While exercising it may be helpful to imagine yourself as a glass of water being emptied and filled. When the water is poured out, the glass empties from the top to the bottom. When the water is poured in, the glass fills from the bottom to the top.

★ The best time to do these exercises is in the morning. That is the time when you are fresh and your nerve centres are alert ★

The technique is a simple one: assume a simple and relaxed standing posture. Try inhaling, filling the lower lungs first, then the middle lungs, and then, finally, the upper lungs; simultaneously, raise the arms until they are overhead, with hands joined together in a prayer position.

Then exhale, emptying the upper lungs first, then the middle lungs, and then the lower lungs; simultaneously, lower the arms back to the side.

Repeat the exercise two to five more times.

Exercise 2: *Diaphragmatic breathing*

Although breathing is one of the most vital functions, it is little understood and often done improperly. Most people breathe shallowly and haphazardly, going against the natural rhythmic movement of the body's respiratory system.

Diaphragmatic breathing, on the other hand, promotes a natural, smooth breath movement that strengthens the nervous system and relaxes the body. The importance of deep, even breathing in meditation cannot be overemphasised.

Respiration is normally of either one of two types, or a combination of both: chest or abdominal. Chest breathing or shallow breathing is characterised by an outward movement of the upper chest. Deep abdominal breathing is characterised by an outward movement of the abdominal wall due to the contraction and descent of the diaphragm. Practitioners of yoga recognise a third type of breathing, known as diaphragmatic breathing, which focusses attention on the diaphragm in the lower rib cage. It is this method of breathing that is practised during the asana. Remember, diaphragmatic breathing should not be confused with abdominal or belly breathing, which is also sometimes referred to as deep diaphragmatic breathing.

The principal muscle of diaphragmatic breathing, the diaphragm, is a strong, horizontal, dome-shaped muscle. It divides the thoracic cavity, which contains the heart and lungs, from the abdominal cavity, which contains the organs of digestion, reproduction and excretion. The diaphragm is located approximately at mid-chest, in its relaxed dome-shaped state.

During inhalation, the diaphragm contracts and flattens; it gets pushed downwards, causing the upper abdominal muscles to relax and extend slightly and the lower 'floating' ribs to flare slightly outward. In this position the lungs expand, creating a partial vacuum, which draws air into the chest cavity. During exhalation, the diaphragm relaxes and returns to its dome-shaped position. During this upward movement, the upper abdominal muscles contract and carbon dioxide is forced from the lungs.

Although breathing is one of the most vital functions, it is little understood and often done improperly

Diaphragmatic breathing has three important effects on the body:

1. Unlike shallow breathing, the lungs are filled completely, providing the body with sufficient oxygen.

2. The waste products of the respiratory process and carbon dioxide are forced out from the lungs. When breathing shallowly, a bit of carbon dioxide may remain trapped in the lungs, thereby causing some amount of fatigue and nervousness.

3. The up-and-down motion of the diaphragm gently massages the abdominal organs; this increases circulation to these organs and thus aids in their functioning.

In diaphragmatic breathing, a minimal effort is used to receive a large amount of air, hence it is the most efficient method.

The technique here is to lie on the back, keeping the feet apart at a comfortable distance. Gently close the eyes and place one hand on the upper abdomen and the other on the chest. Inhale and exhale through the nostrils slowly, smoothly and evenly, with no noise, jerks or pauses in the breath. While inhaling, be aware of the upper abdominal muscles expanding and the lower ribs flaring out slightly. There should be little or no movement of the chest.

Follow this method of deep breathing for three to five minutes daily until you clearly understand the movement of the diaphragm and the upper abdominal muscles. The body is designed to breathe diaphragmatically; gradually it should again become a natural function.

There is a delightful story by Susan Kramer of nine-year-old twins and their experience of deep breathing. Anneke and Hans lived in Holland, a beautiful village with wooded parks and canals. One exceptionally windy day, on their way back from a difficult day at school, they stopped by at a pretty little wood. Here there were tall trees with birds huddled together. Anneke started imitating the whooshing sound of the wind by breathing in and out in an even manner. She urged Hans to join her and together they started copying the sound of the wind and enjoyed doing it.

Suddenly they realised that they were feeling much better and that the stress they had felt just a short while ago had vanished. They were full of fresh energy. Breathing in and out in a regulated manner continuously had helped Anneke and Hans to rid their minds of the worries that they were carrying home from school. Unwittingly they had come across an exercise that was comforting.

> Deep breathing relaxes your nerves and meditation helps your mind to unwind

Deep breathing is always a good relaxation exercise and helps to still the mind. It is a very effective precursor to meditation. In fact some use it along with meditation by telling themselves, "I am" as they breathe in and "relax" as they breathe out. This way you discipline your body to respond to the breathing exercises that you have learnt and you get to meditate as well. The deep breathing relaxes your nerves and the meditation helps your mind to unwind. As a result both your mind and your body get a rest. You are totally refreshed and ready to take on the world again.

A study conducted by Ron Mangun, Director of the Center for Mind and Brain at the University of California, USA, found that when you do three months of continuous and thorough training in deep breathing, it allows you to let all thoughts leave your mind. There is a noticeable change in how your brain becomes more attentive. The action of telling your mind to release the thoughts that clutter it helps the brain to attend to other happenings in your life. The study provides further neuroscience evidence of changes that take place in the brain with meditation. We can see that, with the practice of meditation, we can improve all aspects of our functioning.

Advance Slowly

Whichever method you opt for, the meditation habit is certainly one worth developing. It results in a life of alert and joyful tranquillity. As a beginner it is best not to over extend yourself. Concentrate on the quality of the meditation rather than the quantity. Do not meditate for so long that you go off to sleep at the end of it. That would be a total waste for the meaning of meditation is to awaken your senses and make you more alert, not to lull you to sleep. As you get used to meditating, the quality will improve. The time will naturally become longer then.

Remember never to do any meditation on your bed. That is the place meant for you to sleep. It should stay that way. However tempting it may be to sit on the bed and begin your daily meditation routine, do not do so. The results certainly will not be either up to your expectations or up to the potential that they promise. Avoid that first impulse to laziness. It requires only a little will power and you will surely get the best results.

Willing yourself to get up and get going is the first step to the successful practice and joy of meditation. You will always congratulate yourself once you are firmly into the practice of meditation.

A good test to see that your meditation is effective and progressing well is when your meditation is long but you feel that you have spent very little time on it.

★ Concentrate on the quality of the meditation rather than the quantity ★

That is true of so many other positive things in life, too. The good times seem to pass very quickly and the bad times linger on. Surely you would like to be part of the good times—just allow meditation to lead you there.

Way 6

Control your breath

Meditation improves with conscious breathing

| Chapter Seven |

Focus Your Mind

The more man meditates upon good thoughts, the better will be his world and the world at large.

Confucius

Concentration helps us in many ways. It assists us in grasping quickly what another person says, it increases our ability to remember things, it helps us to focus on our goals and achieve them more easily. Concentration, you will find, so focusses your mind that solutions come surprisingly fast and easily—they almost flow into you. And to imagine that you can reap these benefits only by thinking intensively for a few minutes makes the whole process even more rewarding.

As a child you may have tried the experiment of directing the sun's rays on a piece of paper through a magnifying glass. If the paper was too close to the magnifying glass or too far, nothing happened. It had to be at exactly the right point to burn. So, too, with concentration. If used correctly it helps you to take charge of your life.

There is the famous story from the Indian epic, *The Mahabharata*. Arjuna was competing with other princes and noblemen. It was a test of archery; the target was the fish rotating above. The catch was to hit the target as it was reflected in a huge cauldron of water below. All others looked in the direction of the fish, saw it rotate and tried to shoot their arrow into it. But Arjuna focussed on a small area. He focussed only on the eye of the fish with all his concentration. Arjuna's arrow left its bow and pierced the eye of the fish. That is the secret of concentration. Once you have developed the ability to concentrate, your mind becomes your slave—you can tell it to do exactly what you want. You can throw out all negative thoughts and focus only on positive ones. You can decide to be with people who make you happy and comfortable and stay away from those who are complex and difficult to deal with. You can look for work that interests you rather than slog away at things that are boring and dreary. Regular meditation helps you to acquire this ability.

> ★ Concentration, you will find, so focusses your mind that solutions come surprisingly fast and easily ★

Keep at it

Patanjali, the great Indian sage who lived around 500 BC, wrote a treatise on life, in which he explains that when the mind is still, the real self, which is our higher consciousness, comes to the forefront. It is a gradual process that takes place over many years of application. Do not expect results overnight. You have to keep at it and remember that as you progress your connection with your inner self will get better. Your ability to understand what you like and what you dislike will sharpen. You will be more in control of your thoughts—something that you perhaps never imagined was possible.

Patanjali's treatise consists of hundred-and-ninety-six brief statements called sutras. In this classic text, aptly called *The Yoga Sutras,* meaning the knowledge of union, are profound metaphysical concepts condensed to their seed form. They describe the whole process we call life, why we suffer and how we can return to and live in the blissful and natural state of our real self. This great work pierces the veil of illusion and provides a peep into reality.

Presented below are a few selected sutras from Patanjali's work, to show how, with brilliant economy and intellect, the meditator can achieve a blissful state of enlightenment:

Sutra 2: *Yoga is the cessation of the modifications of the mind*
Cessations refer to the end or the stilling of different types of thought waves, or anything that disturbs the mind's stillness.

Sutra 3: *Then the Seer is established in his own essential nature*
When there are no thought waves, the Seer attains self-realisation and starts living in harmony with his or her real and natural self.

Sutra 4: *In other states there is assimilation of the Seer with the modifications of the mind*
When we are not living according to our true nature, we identify ourselves with our thoughts. But since our thoughts are largely conditioned by our past circumstances, they are not the real us.

The Last Sutra: This sutra states that the final stage of meditation produces enlightenment, and this occurs only when we are living according to our real nature, which is pure consciousness.

Patanjali does not recommend the need to suppress your thoughts. Trying to still the mind forcibly never works and, in fact, creates greater problems. All the Seers agree that there are only two ways to reduce thought waves. One is to observe your thoughts passively by detaching yourself from them. The other is through meditation when you focus or concentrate on the mind.

★ Once you have developed the ability to concentrate, your mind becomes your slave ★

Be focussed on whatever it is that you want in your life. Concentrate on whatever it is that you feel requires your attention to better your sense of self-worth and happiness. Indeed, concentration is the key to your well-being.

Way 7

Be focussed

Meditation helps you to take charge of your life

|Chapter Eight|

Discover Yourself

Meditation brings wisdom; lack of meditation leads to ignorance. Know well what leads you forward and what holds you back, and choose the path that leads to wisdom.

The Buddha

The scientific technique of meditation helps us to observe the nature of our minds and arrive at the truth of suffering within—how we are agitated, what it is that irritates us and what makes us miserable. In the scriptures and in the words of the awakened spiritual Masters, the mind has often been described as a monkey intoxicated with alcohol, or even as a wild horse that we need to tame. Apt metaphors indeed, but to understand this truth about the nature of your own mind you need to go deep within yourself to observe this truth objectively and honestly.

Meditation teaches you to just observe. For example, if you are miserable, just observe the misery as misery, without feeling compelled to do anything about it. As you start observing, the cause of misery becomes clear because you are reacting with negativity, craving or aversion. But as you keep observing that sensation, it loses its strength and passes away. And the negativity passes with it.

Meditation also shows you why you feel the way you feel, how you have become what you are and the repeated patterns of behaviour that you are conditioned to operate under without awareness. The goal of meditation is not to achieve just another transitory 'other-worldly' experience, but to accept whatever manifests itself with equanimity and ease. This way, mental conditioning is eradicated layer by layer and along with it suffering is removed.

The ego, in its own respect, has convinced us that we desperately need it. In fact it goes beyond—not only that we need the ego, but also that we are it. "I am my body. I am my feelings. I am my thoughts. I am my personality. I am suppressed. I am sincere and honest"—all these are the earnest pleadings of the ego.

★ Meditation shows you why you feel the way you feel, how you have become what you are ★

The mind is like a camera: it creates, perceives and records reality. Its depth is unfathomable, its breadth unimaginable and its energy boundless. Meditation, which takes you beyond the mind, raises the question, "Who am I really?" The powers of the mind should be concentrated and turned back upon itself. Only then will it penetrate into its own innermost secrets, as it is the darkest places that reveal their secrets to the penetrating rays of the sun.

We shall then perceive for ourselves whether or not we have souls, whether or not life exists for five minutes or for eternity. And whether or not there is a universal consciousness.

Relax Your Mind

As the wise say, the proof of the pudding is in the eating and in this chain of thought we must never discount something as untrue before actually trying it out for ourselves. Scientists like to define meditation as a state of restful alertness in which the mind is relaxed, yet alert. It is often called the meditative state of consciousness because it is different from our normal waking and sleeping consciousness.

Since the mind is the source of happiness or unhappiness, stress or mental composure, sickness or well-being, failure or success, it is only logical that we should direct our attention to the mind. Even doctors admit that at least seventy per cent of physical diseases are psychosomatic, that is, they originate in the mind. So for every ten people who declare themselves sick, seven suffer from illnesses that begin in the mind, whether triggered by fear, worry, anger, jealousy or any other negative emotion.

Stay Calm

Once you begin meditating, you become more peaceful, less reactive and more stable—all these states bring greater efficiency to your life. Anxiety and panic are a waste of energy. Tense muscles, overactive nerves and an overactive mind drain our energy reserves. Becoming calm rejuvenates us once again. Calmness and vitality are complementary. People who are 'hyper' may seem energetic but they are actually fuelled by nervous energy. They end up being irritable and mentally exhausted when their nervous energy wears off. You can feel the beneficial effects of meditation right after the few initial sessions. The early results are subtle but cumulative. So, with every passing day you will find yourself a little less stressed, a little happier and a little closer to your goal. My advice to you is, try meditation; it has to work.

★ Scientists like to define meditation as a state of restful alertness in which the mind is relaxed, yet alert ★

As you extend the time you spend meditating, the requirements of both your body and your mind will keep changing. The challenges that you will be able to take up will become greater and very soon the skill of meditation will turn into an art. It will flow so easily that you will be able to enjoy it immensely. And, like the circle of life, one challenge will lead to another, making life more beautiful and meaningful than ever before.

Seven Techniques to Meditate Anywhere, Anytime

Though there are literally thousands of techniques that you can use when you decide to meditate, I am giving you seven that are very simple and can be used at any level of proficiency. The practice will require anywhere from a few seconds of your time to about 30 minutes, depending upon what technique you choose to use. I encourage you to remember that the purpose of meditation is initially to bring one-pointedness and focus to the mind and then to lead the mind to become still.

When the mind becomes still, you will see deeper into the depth of your own soul. And it is here that you will know your inherent, eternal truth. Pick any technique to begin with, practise it and then experiment with the others. Soon you will have a greater understanding of which one is better for you. Once you find the one you are drawn to, stick to that. Remember to infuse your practice with discipline, devotion and dedication. Though there are numerous ways to meditate, only one technique is required to take you to the end. Find the one for you and use it as your path to the destination.

1. STOP! Say, "stop!" to yourself many times in a day. Become aware of your thought at that point in time and simply watch it for a few seconds. This deceptively simple technique requires only a few seconds to practise, but leads to tremendous insights. With regular practise you become aware of the in-disciplined tendency of the mind to constantly focus on the negatives.

2. Mindfulness At every moment give the action you are involved in (walking, eating, reading, gardening and so on) your full attention. Your mind should be totally absorbed in the action. Being of full-mind is called mindfulness. This technique can be practised no matter what activity you are engaged in.

3. Ana-Pana Sati This is one of the simplest techniques to practise and has unbelievable positive effects on the

system. Keep your attention focussed on your breath and allow the breath to come into your body and leave your body as it pleases. Allow the breath cycle to be completely natural. Just put your attention fully on the inflow and outflow of your breath and keep it there.

4. 4-2-6 Breath With your mind fully on your breath, breathe in to a count of four, retain to a count of two and breathe out to a count of six. Repeat this with a full mind for about five minutes. Then relax into your natural state of breath.

5. Mantra Recitation Many times during the day, reaffirm silently to yourself, "I am Whole" or "I am Love". Feel the emotion of your mantra totally. Become one with it.

6. Contemplation Take a spiritual word and contemplate its inner meaning and significance in your life. Keep all your thoughts centred on that one concept or idea.

7. Concentration Place your attention on any one colour, object, sound or word. If your mind shifts, bring it back.

(For a complete listing of the meditations offered by Vikas Malkani, visit www.soulcentre.org)

Way 8

Be upbeat

Meditation makes you aware
of who you are

|Chapter Nine|

See the Reality

Meditation is the dissolution of thoughts in eternal awareness or pure consciousness without objectification, knowing without thinking, merging finitude in infinity.

Sivananda

A peaceful life is what all human beings are meant to live. It is just that we get so embroiled in our day-to-day concerns, worries, regrets and guilt that we forget this fundamental reality. We waste far too much energy on things that are not a reflection of the real world and, in the process, become so accustomed to the negative state of mind that we assume they make up our reality.

This reality then begins to pervade our inner being and negatively affects our thoughts, our actions and our relationships. If we are not trained or fortunate enough to be led out of this, we would make this negative reality our own to the exclusion of positive impulses, feelings and emotions. We will be irritable and tense all the time.

We also do not realise that there are many ways of achieving a calm and serene life. This reality emerges only when our higher consciousness is allowed to shine through and that is possible if we are able to still the mind through meditation. All through our lives we carry with us two heavy burdens—the thoughts and regrets of the past and the worries and expectations of the future. At each and every moment, these burdens weigh us down. Meditation allows us to see the reality and to take a rest from following our deeply ingrained and conditioned patterns of behaviour.

★ We do not realise that there are many ways of achieving a calm and serene life ★

Meditation, many believe, is not a way to make things easier; it is a way to make them real, so that one will have to grow in the process. What meditation does is make you more sensitive and aware. And, if you have a painful problem in your life, meditation will probably make it more painful because it will make you more sensitive and force you to accept the truth.

Meditation will not let you hide from the pain any more. It will compel you to step right in the middle of it and face it. No more can issues be avoided or simply wished away. They must be accepted fully and then the choice of what you wish your future to be must be exercised. It can be of benefit in many ways, particularly in strengthening or raising awareness.

Meditation is not some sort of panacea. It is a direct and powerful way to engage in your own growth and evolution. And, as is often the case, growth is painful. It hurts! But growth is the natural process of life. We need to nurture it, however, with positive energies. If you opt to do this through the techniques of meditation you will be able to achieve your life goals more easily and in a more enduring manner.

Reincarnate Yourself

Genuine meditation involves a whole series of deaths and rebirths and strong stresses and conflicts may come into play. All of this is balanced by an equal growth in compassion, equanimity, understanding, awareness, sensitivity and the ability to let go, which makes the whole effort worthwhile and productive. The lives of most of the great saints and sages, from all cultures, show tremendous growth and change when they have progressed in meditation. There are both extraordinary benefits and extraordinary pains on this path to your own reality and truth.

Meditation leads you to understand the nature of your mind, master it, and then to rise above it. With the regular practice of meditation the mind becomes one-pointed and still, instead of constantly being restless. As the mind becomes calm, you gain more and more control over your ability to direct it to a specific task. Meditation, in fact, introduces you to your own inherent reality and makes you the master of yourself.

Go Beyond Contemplation

There is another step in the evolution of the self from a state of stress and tension to that of bliss and tranquillity. This is described as contemplation. It is often practised by many as they learn concentration. Contemplation, especially the contemplation of inspiring concepts or ideals, such as truth, peace and love, can be very helpful, although it is distinct and different from the process of meditation. While contemplating, you engage your mind in inquiring into the lives of saints, sages and great thinkers. You can also dwell on ideas and concepts that have been developed and refined by these superior beings. In your contemplation of such concepts you may take into consideration new meanings, values and insights.

In the system of meditation, contemplation is considered a separate practice, one that can be very useful at times. When you engage yourself in meditation, you do not ask the mind to think or contemplate on any concept; instead, you allow it to go beyond this level of mental activity.

Explore Your Deeper Levels

★ Meditation, many believe, is not a way to make things easier; it is a way to make them real ★

In hypnosis, a suggestion is made to the mind, either by another person or by your own self. Such suggestions may take the form of, "You are feeling sleepy (or relaxed)." Thus in hypnosis there is an attempt to program, manipulate or control the content of the mind to make it believe a certain fact, or think in an ordered, particular way. Sometimes, such powerful suggestions can be very useful.

Unfortunately, negative suggestions have negative effects on us and on our health. In meditation, you do not make any attempts to give the mind a direct suggestion or to control the mind. You simply observe and let the mind become quiet and calm, allowing your mantra (if that be your technique of choice) to lead you deeper within, exploring and experiencing the deeper levels of your being.

Know Yourself

The fastest path to understanding your mind and knowing yourself is through the practice of meditation. Meditation is ancient all right, but contrary to popular belief, it is totally non-religious, very scientific and an empowering technique that is unmatched.

Meditation never asks what our faith or belief is: whether we are atheists, Christians, Buddhists, Muslim or Hindus. As long as we are human beings we can attain self-awareness through meditation. The fact that it has not just existed but thrived for almost ten thousand years and been used by not only spiritual Masters but also common folk all over the world speaks volumes for its credibility.

Meditation is not some strange or foreign technique that requires you to change beliefs, your culture or religion. Meditation is not a religious ritual or practice at all; rather, it is a very practical, scientific and systematic technique for knowing yourself at all levels. Meditation does not 'belong to' any culture or religion of the world. Meditation is not the preserve of any group or sect of people either. It is humankind's common inheritance across all regions and civilisations. Religion teaches you what to believe in, but meditation teaches you to experience your beliefs directly for yourself. There is no conflict between the techniques of religion and meditation. You can practise one without the other or both together, as you choose.

★ Meditation leads you to understand the nature of your mind, master it, and then to rise above it ★

Worship is a part of the religious system, as is prayer, which is a dialogue with the divine principle. Certainly, you can be both a religious person who prays and a meditator who uses the techniques of meditation, but it is not necessary to have an orthodox religion to meditate. Meditation should be used as a pure technique, in a systematic, orderly way.

Meditation makes no demands on you except that of making you face up to your own self. In the beginning this process may disrupt what you consider an orderly way of living. However, the discomfort will soon pass and your bond with yourself and the levels of your own consciousness will be strengthened and enriched.

Way 9

Open your mind

Meditation allows you to evolve constantly

| Chapter Ten |

Stop Worrying

When I meditate, I clearly see that God is already seated inside my heart.

Sri Chinmoy

It is true that meditation helps you to connect with yourself. It brings you closer to what your real or natural self is meant to be. It helps you to become a better listener and to think clearly. There is no one who would want to live a life full of worries. So, actually, meditation provides you the key to happiness. The more you meditate and look within, the more your ability to tackle your worries is likely to be. Go ahead and empower yourself. All you need is to decide that it is your worries that you want to get rid of.

When you start to think of the future and are on the brink of anxiety, also say to yourself, "We'll see." Two small words, but they are powerful and can prevent a lot of worrying. You do not know what is going to happen tomorrow or later in life, so why worry right now about what might or might not happen.

We worry because it is a habit and the best way to break the habit is to replace worrying thoughts with a positive expression. The reason why this technique works so well is because the vast majority of our worries never actually happen. That is a fact. Even though they are a figment of our imagination, they cause a lot of distress, accompanied with health problems and premature ageing. Since, in general, worries do not manifest themselves, it is pointless to worry. By saying "We'll see" every time you think of some possible future event, the mind will eventually give up worrying, since it has learned not to project itself into the future. The other way meditation works is based on the fact that whatever we think about, we tend to attract. In other words, what we fear, we attract. This is especially so if we keep worrying about the same thing. This principle feeds on repetition. But by replacing a worry with "We'll see", we are no longer giving power to that worry nor are we encouraging that worry in any way.

★ The more you meditate and look within, the more your ability to tackle your worries is likely to be ★

A good expression to replace worry is "Forget the results". If you are in business and are worrying about how work will go this week, replace that worry with the thought, "Forget the results". Application of efforts is the cause of success. Or, as Dale Carnegie said, "If you can't sleep, then get up and do something instead of lying there and worrying. It's the worry that gets you, not the loss of sleep." For example, if you are working on a project and are worried about the results, you are not applying a hundred per cent concentration that the project deserves. Worries make you omit things and commit mistakes. Concentrate on what you are doing. If you do the right things and put in your best, then the results will take care of themselves.

This expression gives us great relief, since we can now focus on the application of efforts and stop wasting time worrying about the results. What we can take responsibility for, however, is to change our state of mind. This, according to Buddhism, is the most significant thing that we can do. It is, in fact, the only positive way to handle worry, anxiety, confusion and hatred. Meditation helps us to transform the mind. Whatever technique we choose, meditation develops concentration and clarity in our minds. With regular practice, a pattern develops. We then get used to thinking in a calm, positive and peaceful way. We become more disciplined and we learn to be patient. Reaching such a state energises our mind and can transform us in a considerable way.

Wang Wei, the eighth century Chinese painter, musician and poet, explains this beautifully: "...Mountains and rivers are in the Buddha's eye, the universe in dharma's body. Don't be surprised that meditation controls hot days and raises wind over the land."

For each of us, life has to take a certain course and it will. A positive attitude will take us a long way in this journey of life, as this story points out: Two monks came to a shallow river and were about to cross when they noticed a young woman. She explained to them that she was too scared to walk across the river. One of the monks said, "Don't worry, I'll take you across." He picked her up in his arms and carried her across.

After the monks had continued their journey for some time, the other monk said, "You should not have taken that young lady in your arms across the river; you know we are forbidden contact with women."

The monk replied, "I let go of that woman after crossing the river bank; you're still carrying her."

This story further emphasises the point that once you have made a decision and acted on it, there is no point in finding faults with it later. So stop brooding on it and carry on with life. Make it pleasant and peaceful. If worries come along, the technique is to just observe them as worries and nothing else. Do not use up your energy to think about worries. Use it, instead, to think about strengthening your mind to tackle these worries.

> Whatever technique we choose, meditation develops concentration and clarity in our minds

Meditation will help you to face your worries and deal with them. It is a powerful tool to handle your problems, for it will compel you to deal with the difficulties directly. And, once that is done, you will be free to move ahead, evolve and grow as a productive and positive person.

Meditation as a Process

In the process of meditation, we ask the mind to let go of its tendencies to think, analyse, remember, solve problems and focus on the events of the past or on the expectations of the future. We help the mind to slow down its rapid series of thoughts and feelings and to replace that mental activity with an inner awareness and attention. While meditating, we try to let go of all the mental distractions, preoccupations and the fleeting thoughts and associations of our normal waking experience. We do this, not by trying to make the mind empty, which is impossible, but instead, by allowing the mind to focus on one subtle element or object, which leads the attention further inwards. By giving the mind an internal focus of attention, we help it to refrain from other stressful mental processes, such as worrying, planning, thinking and reasoning.

Osho, the Indian spiritual Master, captures the essence of meditation superbly when he says, "Meditation is not something that you do. It is, only when your doer has gone and you are totally relaxed and not doing anything, in a deep state of let-go, rest—there is meditation. Then meditation flowers. It is the flowering of your being."

Thus, meditation is not thinking about problems or analysing a situation. It is not fantasising or daydreaming or merely letting the mind wander aimlessly. Meditation is simply a quiet, effortless, one-point focus of attention and awareness that opens your mind to new experiences.

Discipline Yourself

> While meditating, we try to let go of all the mental distractions

Meditation can be very frustrating at first. Most beginners find themselves thinking about daily problems and worries when trying to meditate, instead of clearing their minds and enjoying the state of calmness. Sometimes you can even get bored when trying to still your mind and wonder whether all this is really worth it. Do not give up. Just as you keep striving for so many wonderful things in life, you must keep trying to discipline yourself in order to meditate. With time you will definitely be better. You will then enjoy the meditation process.

The key to the regularity of meditation is to choose a time that you are comfortable with. Take a look at what a typical day is like for you. If you are out for most of the day, you may want to do your meditation just before you leave the house or perhaps soon after you bathe. Plan your day in such a way that you can factor in all your essential activities as well as keep time for your meditation. You will never regret it.

Way 10

Let go

Meditation helps you to face your worries and cope with them

| Chapter Eleven |

Turn Stress to Strength

I have brought myself, by long meditation, to the conviction that a human being with a settled purpose must accomplish it and that nothing can resist a will which will stake even existence upon its fulfilment.

Benjamin Disraeli

We all go through many changes in life and in trying to come to terms with these we accumulate a lot of stress along the way. Meditation is a sure way to deal with various forms of stress. It also depends a lot on how you think. If you decide that stress can be tackled by turning it into a strength, you would be able to achieve a great deal in life. And decide is all you have to do. It requires will power but it is not impossible to achieve.

The Dalai Lama who once watched a brain surgery asked the surgeons who were performing it whether the mind can shape brain matter. The scientists explained to him that mental experiences do actually show chemical and electrical changes in the brain—when electrical impulses zip through our visual cortex, for instance, we see; when neurochemicals course through the limbic system, we feel.

But the Dalai Lama was not convinced. He wanted to know if it could work the other way round. "In addition to the brain giving rise to thoughts and hopes and beliefs and emotions that add up to this thing we call the mind, maybe the mind also acts back on the brain to cause physical changes in the very matter that created it. If so, then pure thought would change the brain's activity, its circuits or even its structure," he queried.

The Dalai Lama, by his sensitivity to the human condition and by his long training and practise of meditation, had grasped, almost by instinct, an extremely fundamental question on contemporary knowledge and research on the brain and how it functions.

★ If you decide that stress can be tackled by turning it into a strength, you would be able to achieve a great deal in life ★

In order to find out what changes take place in the brain during meditation, the Dalai Lama sent monks and lamas who had practised meditation for at least ten thousand hours to Professor Richard Davidson at the University of Wisconsin, USA.

As the volunteers began meditating, one kind of brain wave grew unusually strong: gamma waves. Some of the novices "showed a slight but significant increase in the gamma signal," explained the professor.

There was just one exception. Between meditations, the gamma signal in the monks never died down. Even when they were not meditating, their brains were different from those of the novices as they were marked by waves associated with perception, problem-solving and consciousness. The more hours of meditation training a monk undertook, the more enduring was the gamma signal.

The differences noticed between the monks and the novices were interesting. In each case, the monks with the most hours of meditation showed the most dramatic brain changes. That was a strong hint that mental training makes it easier for the brain to turn on circuits that underlie compassion and empathy.

"This positive state is a skill that can be trained," according to Professor Davidson. "Our findings clearly indicate that meditation can change the function of the brain in an enduring way," he elaborated.

The Dalai Lama's line of thought shows a profound impact on the transformation of mental, physical and emotional tension into energy that is creative and effective. To this you must add your own common sense strategies. Here are twenty-five simple methods that you can use:

1. Take time to be alone on a regular basis, listen to your heart, check your intentions, re-evaluate your goals and your activities.

2. Simplify your life! Start eliminating the trivial things that you experience. Do not think too much about the minor things in life.

3. Take a deep breath as often as you can, especially while on the phone, in the car, or waiting for something or someone. Use every opportunity to relax and revitalise yourself.

★ Simplify your life! Start eliminating the trivial things ★

4. Each day, plan to do something that brings you joy, something that you love to do, something done just for yourself.

5. When you are concerned about something, talk it over with someone you trust, or write down your feelings.

6. Say 'No' in a firm but kind way when asked to do something you really do not want to do.

7. Exercise regularly! Stretching your body releases tension. It helps you to relax.

8. Remember, it takes less energy to get an unpleasant task done 'right then' than to worry about it all day.

9. Take time to be with nature, people you like and children. Even in the city, noticing the seasonal changes or watching people's faces can be a good harmoniser.

10. Consciously teach yourself to do one thing at a time, keeping your mind focussed on the present. Do whatever

you are doing slowly, more intentionally and with more awareness and respect.

11. Choose not to waste your precious present life being guilty about the past or being concerned about the future.

12. Learn a variety of relaxation techniques and practise at least one, regularly. Even when you are in the car, travelling to work, or stuck in a terrible traffic jam, treat this as a good time to meditate, provided you do not have to drive, of course.

13. When you find yourself angry in situations, instead of fighting it ask yourself, "What can I learn from this?" Anyone or anything that makes you angry is showing you how you let yourself be controlled by your expectations of how someone or something should be. When you accept yourself, others and the various situations for what they are, you become more effective in influencing people whom you meet to change according to your wishes.

14. Become more aware of the demands you place on yourself, your environment and on others just in order to be different from how they are at any moment. Remember, demands are tremendous sources of stress; therefore, be more reasonable in your demands and reduce stress.

15. If you have a hectic schedule, prioritise your activities and do the most important ones first.

16. Take frequent breaks to relax.

★ Become more aware of the demands you place on yourself, your environment ★

17. Organise your life in such a manner as to include time for fun and spontaneity. Set a realistic schedule, allowing some transition time between activities. Eliminate unnecessary commitments.

18. Laugh, smile, stop worrying and be happy—in other words, treat yourself as a very important person who deserves to get the best in life.

19. Learn to delegate responsibility.

20. Monitor your intake of sugar, salt, caffeine and alcohol. The correct diet is imperative. Often we tend to neglect this aspect of our lives till we have a health problem.

21. Create and maintain a personal support system—people with whom you can afford to be vulnerable.

22. Be more kind to yourself and to others.

23. Welcome change as an opportunity and a challenge to learn and grow.

24. Watch the clouds or the waves on water. Listen to music or to the sounds around you. Notice the silence between the sounds and the space between the objects.

25. In this journey of life, remember to stop and smell the flowers!

If none of these methods work then it just means that you are not being true to yourself and you are not meditating. Andrew Cohen puts it very concisely when he says: "If you're having trouble with meditation that means you're not really doing it. The powerful thing about meditation is its radical simplicity, be still, be at ease, pay attention. That's the beauty of it, meditation means doing absolutely nothing.

"And there are only two positions in relationship to that: you either do it or you don't. But often human beings find this simplicity unbearable. It confronts us with ourselves at the deepest level, and most of us just can't bear that degree of transparency. That's why it's important to learn how to meditate. It is only in the exquisite simplicity of doing absolutely nothing that you begin to be able to see yourself in ways you ordinarily would never be able to do. If you really engage with this unbearable simplicity, it's impossible to hide from yourself."

The advantages of meditation seem to be never-ending. From the time that you begin to take it seriously, the returns that regular meditation brings to you are unimaginable. You will wonder why you had not thought of starting this method earlier. You realise that it is just a technique that needs to be made your own. And yet it is so much more.

★ In this journey of life, remember to stop and smell the flowers ★

With meditation comes good health, inner calmness, peace of mind, even happiness and joy. Meditation is the path that leads you to an abundant, almost carefree life. Your stresses become your strengths; your doubts turn into channels that take you to success.

Way 11

Do one thing at a time

Meditation helps you to simplify your life

| Chapter Twelve |

Heal Yourself

In deep meditation the flow of concentration is continuous like the flow of oil.

Patanjali

In order to facilitate the process of meditation, certain sounds are uttered in a specific sequence. These are called mantras, that is, words, sounds, phrases or simply syllables repeated in order to aid concentration. Repeating mantras leads you to the inner void, the space where the Creator dwells.

Mantras have immense spiritual power as they have been handed down in an oral tradition over thousands of years. Chanting a mantra can be very soothing. It helps both your body and your mind to relax and to forget about your worries and the causes of your stress.

Often, mantras are used during meditation by those who have a problem concentrating and with focussing their minds. The repetition of a mantra is a means of improving the powers of concentration. There are Indian spiritual Masters who maintain that the meaning and the content of the mantra does not necessarily have to be understood by the aspirant in order to bring about the desired effect. Just the recitation of a mantra alone is sufficient to achieve the spiritual awakening, which is its purpose.

Different kinds of mantras are used throughout the world, including Om, Amen and Shalom. They all have a similar goal, which is to help you focus your mind. However, whether ancient or modern, there is a certain method of pronouncing these mantras. Those who are competent in this science can lead students on the right meditative path.

★ Chanting a mantra can be very soothing. It helps both your body and your mind to relax and to forget about your worries ★

Initially the process of meditation is simple and easy to learn, but when one begins to deal with the mind, the prescription of an appropriate mantra has to be done very carefully as it can have an extremely powerful effect. The meditative texts and scriptures speak extensively on this subject. Concentrating on a mantra helps students of meditation to ignore useless, distracting mental worries and proceed into the depths of their inner selves.

Patanjali, the codifier of the science of yoga, speaks of the mantra as a representative of the innermost sources of consciousness. He explains how it acts as a bridge between the mortal and immortal aspects of life. When the body, breath and conscious mind separate from the unconscious mind and the individual soul, the conscious effort of having remembered a mantra continues to create an impression in the unconscious sphere. These impressions are powerful motivators. They help aspirants to confront various situations that arise in their lives.

These could be situations of joy or sorrow. And, so deep and pervasive are the influences of these impressions that they help the aspirant even during the most critical period of transition that we call death. It is said that these powerful motivations make the voyage to the unknown easier and less daunting than it would otherwise appear to be.

Practitioners through the ages have affirmed that the use of a mantra is certain to purify the subconscious. However, each mantra is devotional by nature and has the divine as its form and essence. With concentration on the meaning of the mantra, the attainment of the ultimate goal is surer and quicker. The words, sounds or syllables of the mantra are believed to be so potent that even if it is repeated mechanically some purification will take place.

The benefits of chanting a mantra depend on you as an individual—where you start, where you stand now, what your past life has been and the intensity and degree of longing in your desire. When you chant a mantra, your whole being is transformed. You become a better individual and are able to relate better with yourself and those around you.

Often a meditator will associate a saint or an aspect of God in the form of a deity when chanting a mantra. S/he, while chanting, will give all the emotions to the mantra, to the deity of the mantra and ask that deity to help them gain control of their lives. In this way we find a safe release for negative feelings. Rather than throwing them on someone else, we offer them back to their source. Continued chanting will lead to greater awareness and the replacing of negative feelings with positive affirmations.

Another result that comes quickly with the recitation of a mantra is control of the breath—the means by which we can develop the ability to control our emotions. Mantra practice subdues turbulent emotions and thereby helps to calm the mind.

★ The words, sounds or syllables of the mantra are believed to be so potent that even if it is repeated mechanically some purification will take place ★

In yogic terms there is a difference between emotions and feelings. A true feeling is purified emotion. Mantra yoga, for instance, gives us an opportunity to know our emotions: what they are, where they come from and what their place is in our lives. Through mantra yoga we can learn to manage our emotions to our best advantage. We learn to control and refine our emotions and to encourage the harmonious development of all aspects of the human potential.

As the mantra finds its way into the subconscious, the mind is purified to the extent that we would be incapable of achieving without this aid. Slowly, the ego is overpowered by the higher self. It is like pouring milk into a cup of black coffee until, little by little, the coffee is replaced by pure milk. Even as it purifies the mind, the mantra is a great protection and a barrier from fear. This freedom from fear further unleashes our positive energies and we are well on the path to becoming better individuals.

When emotions are purified they develop into love, which is an important step in the awakening of further levels of consciousness. Thereafter, the influences of the mantra become very subtle. Feelings, which have been purified, bring us into the presence of the divine and from the divine we derive a sense of protection. The mantra is like a shield against all that is negative and disturbing.

The sound of your voice can become an instrument for expressing and controlling your emotions. At times the chanting may be caressing, gentle, intense, full of longing or surrender. If you chant softly, your emotions become softer. They will be refined through the chanting and change into true feelings that are expressed by the heart.

At other times your voice may be strong and powerful, as you put into it all your anger and disappointment, your requests and demands. Honestly express to God what you feel, even your anger and impatience towards the divine, for not bringing you sooner to the light. However, you must guard against emotional self-indulgence while doing so by learning through your practice to control your emotions. In your communion with God this is something that you must never lose sight of. Ultimately you have to assume responsibility for your actions.

Be Humble

When you find that your emotions are beyond control, you may give them back to the divine. You may address the divine at a very personal level, saying, "Why did you give me all these emotions? Why did you not give me the strength and insight to handle them? I want you to come here now and do something about it." This may not seem like a form of prayer, but it is. It is the recognition of the need for help and the willingness to ask God for help and that is humility.

In chanting out the emotions, from the ugliest to the most exalted, and giving them back to the One who gave them to you in the first place, you learn to accept both parts of yourself, the good and the bad, and to transcend the pairs of opposites from which you are trying to free yourself. On the spiritual path, by channelling the emotions towards God, you find that the divine accepts your struggle and aids and sustains you in your search for the ultimate.

> ★ The sound of your voice can become an instrument for expressing and controlling your emotions ★

Emotions in themselves are never bad, but when running wild, they can be extremely damaging. Even love, when not shared or given freely and generously, becomes self-love, which turns back destructively on the individual. When emotions are directed, they are a source of strength for great achievements. Through the power of emotions, men and women have overcome their limitations and attained a higher purpose in life. Emotions, channelled through a mantra towards the divine, can take you closer to God. When chanting a mantra, during meditation, the emotions express themselves in the breath and the voice. Every time the breath is uneven it means that the emotions are involved and we are out of balance. As long as the emotions are running high, this imbalance exists, but gradually they subside and we begin to experience the equilibrium that is our goal.

Chanting helps us to achieve this stillness by bringing the breath and the emotions under control. In these moments of complete stillness of the mind, indescribable bliss is experienced. By repeated practice, it becomes possible to hold on to the contact made with our innermost being.

As the mantras are chanted, moods are brought under control and awareness in the here and now grows. Attention, and therefore energy, is withdrawn from the old thought patterns which, like tapes on a recorder, were playing over and over again. These mental background noises keep us tied to the past and to the future, to fearful imaginings and senseless fantasies, which are the cause of our self-created sufferings.

The ability to concentrate, to achieve single-pointedness and the overcoming of the self go hand-in-hand. Through the practice of mantra and japa yoga, you will find yourself in direct confrontation with the lower self, the ego or the mind. You will become aware of those aspects of your personality that have been in control and have ruled your life. Now, the higher self begins to take possession.

Surrender

To overcome the ego, one must practise surrender. One must be able to surrender to the mantra itself and to the energy of the mantra. Learning to surrender to the mantra and to the energy of the mantra puts in motion the process of purification of the self, by eliminating selfishness, self-glorification, self-justification and self-gratification.

If you go to bed at night and fall asleep with the mantra, it will probably stay with you and you will wake up with it. You will not have nightmares, because the generative power of the mantra dissolves problems and removes the pressures that come from self-importance and self-will.

> ★ The ability to concentrate, to achieve single-pointedness and the overcoming of the self go hand-in-hand ★

Through the use of a mantra during meditation, a greater sensitivity, a refinement of the senses, comes about, which may eventually bring you to the point where you can see with the inner eye and hear with the inner ear. When the inner ear is developed, the music of the spheres may be heard—music of such exquisite beauty as no instrument, no human voice, is able to produce. The cosmic Om might be heard. The impact and the effects of such experiences will bring an intense desire to change for the better. When meditating, remember these six important points:

1. It is a natural, simple, effortless technique for quietening the mind and for revealing the true self. It results in inner peace and happiness.

2. Since the mind is the root cause of stress, failure and unhappiness as well as calmness, success and happiness, it is logical that we should direct our attention to the mind. Meditation has a more powerful and beneficial effect on the mind than any other known activity.

3. It is so simple that anyone can do it. It is also very natural; it requires no drugs or equipment and costs nothing.

4. It is different from relaxation techniques, since it produces a deeper level of relaxation and unfolds our higher consciousness.

5. You will feel the beneficial effects right after your first meditation and, since the effects are cumulative, you will experience increasing benefits as time goes by.

6. It causes you to enjoy everything to a greater extent, including material things, but your happiness no longer

depends on these things, since you are anyway happy from within.

The Results

A mantra is not a magic pill; rather it is like a steady stream of water that gradually wears down the hardest stone.

★ The immediate result of chanting is an increase in the ability to concentrate ★

The immediate result of chanting is an increase in the ability to concentrate, followed gradually by the control of the breath and the emotions. Later the emotions will become refined into true feelings. The most important goal in chanting, however, is the realisation of the self. A mantra will heal you in the most profound manner.

If you choose to take up a mantra you will very soon notice that all the qualities and attributes of the mantra will come to life within you. The spiritual law of "As you think so you become" makes the practitioner literally become what the mantra is.

Way 12

Surrender!

Meditation is the best way to overcome the ego

| Chapter Thirteen |

Enjoy Life

A man of meditation is happy, not for an hour or a day, but quite round the circle of all his years.

Isaac Taylor

Even as a meditator, you can go on liking and owning possessions. But your attitude towards them should be marked by a healthy detachment. Possessions must serve you instead of you serving them. A more serene outlook makes you less disposed to buy things you can ill afford. It stops you from racing to keep up with your neighbour. Your desire for possessions will also decrease if you are at peace within.

When you become less stressed and are living more in tune with your higher consciousness, you enjoy everything more, including material things. Now consider this—if you do not feel good from within, how can you enjoy the material things outside?

The whole basis of meditation is to make you enjoy life more.

The beauty of meditation is that it makes you happy from inside, so you are happy anyway, irrespective of whether you are materialistic or not. Your happiness is not dependent on external factors. So you get not only happiness, but freedom, too. As Richard Carlson says in *What about the Big Stuff?*,

"Meditation is a gift you give to yourself, and I cannot recommend it highly enough. It's a period of time, removed from the busyness, confusion, chaos, noise, and stimulation of the day. It's a time to be quiet and still, tune in, listen, and watch—as the mind does its thing."

★ The whole basis of meditation is to make you enjoy life more ★

In Harmony with Nature

Happiness comes from within, and unless you pay attention to what is within you, you will remain stressed and unhappy, regardless of your economic situation.

Since meditation causes you to connect with your real or natural self, you will gradually feel an increasing desire to live more in harmony with nature.

You will also tend to gravitate towards a simpler lifestyle without extra or unnecessary burdens. You will desire more natural things such as nourishing food, fresh air and exercise. If you smoke or drink alcohol excessively, your taste for these vices will diminish. You will stop overeating.

Meditation causes your innate intelligence and life force to manifest itself more strongly. This results in an urge to live more in accordance with nature's laws. Since your mind is less cluttered with unnecessary thoughts, you get more focussed and your goals are clarified.

Improve Your Relationships

Meditation has a powerful effect on relationships of all kinds. Our relationships with other people also improve. We cease to worry about others hurting us. In any case, we tend to attract those who can contribute to our lives in ways of wisdom and abundance.

When our mind calms down and our higher consciousness starts expressing itself, we become less subjective and more objective. The process of meditation both calms our senses and sharpens them.

As our ability to be rational and realistic is emphasised and increased, our judgements become better, leading to more self-confident actions. We perceive the reality of our relationships more profoundly than ever before and this leads to a calmness that pervades our entire being.

So, in one word, meditate. It will connect you to yourself as well as to others and the divine within you. Once you start seeing oneness everywhere, you will find yourself in harmony with the people around you, you will find that life becomes that much more fun.

I have noticed that life is beautiful when you opt to live in a state of meditation. Suddenly, the grass looks greener, the sun shines brighter and yes, the coffee, too, smells better. To enjoy life, you *have* to meditate. There is no getting out of this one. Choose your time, your method, even your company (some people enjoy meditating in a group, others look at it as an intense and very private affair). But just be at it.

All great Masters have spent their lives in joyful meditation. For them, every act is a form of meditation. Their lives are a long series of meditations; that is their reality.

★ When our mind calms down and our higher consciousness starts expressing itself, we become less subjective and more objective ★

Make it yours and reap the benefits. As I have always emphasised, meditation is not a destination. It is the journey itself; a joyful path that invariably leads you to self-realisation and enlightenment.

Way 13

Be yourself

Meditation improves your relationships

|Chapter Fourteen|

Reach Out

Prayer is when you talk to God; meditation is when you listen to God.

Diana Robinson

Meditation is a very powerful technique that has tremendous healing powers and is your path to a higher level of consciousness. It helps you to see calmly and correctly the various aspects of your life—your relationships, your career, your ambitions and your duties as a human being.

But in order to listen you have to first learn to be quiet. For many, therefore, prayer precedes meditation. We have spoken to God through our prayers and now we give God the opportunity to enter our lives and to speak to us. This is meditation. God comforts and heals us as we meditate. God shows us the path that we need to see at that moment.

Therefore, make time to listen to God. This is a very important communion, one that brings you closest to becoming one with the universe. These moments are not easy to come by. You must *want* these moments and you must *strive* for them. Remember that meditation can help you arrive at this. You have the examples and the experiences of sages and wise men and others who have trod the path before you. There is a very powerful message in meditation. Whether you do so individually, or in a group, you are never alone. For instance, if you are having problems in the family and you find it difficult to share these with an outsider, you could turn to meditation for help. In fact, the entire family could take up meditation together.

★ God comforts and heals us as we meditate. God shows us the path that we need to see at that moment ★

Be Compassionate

Calming down and soothing yourself, which happens as a result of meditation, will almost instantly lead to an emergence of compassion and kindness to those around you. This will, in turn, help you to observe your family in a new light. You will begin to see the positive aspects of others. Some of these traits may never have been noticed by you before. Meditation brings you closer to others. Try it. Do not dismiss it. Attempt to make this connection. You will be rewarded with greater tranquillity.

Pray for Others

There is a well-known study by cardiologist Randolph Bryd of the San Francisco General Hospital who decided to research the efficacy of prayer. He took five hundred patients who had been admitted to the coronary intensive care unit, either for the treatment of heart attack or for ruling out heart attack, and had them randomly assigned to a 'prayed-for' and a 'not-prayed-for' group. It was the pinnacle of controlled scientific research—a randomised double-blind study. None of the staff knew who was in which group, so they could not preferentially give care to one group and not the other and the subjects were chosen at random. Therefore, factors such as sex, age, health and demographics balanced out. Dr Bryd then farmed out their names to prayer groups of various denominations around the country.

When they broke the code at the end of the study, they found that indeed the 'prayed-for' patients did significantly better on a number of measures. They got fewer infections, needed fewer antibiotics and got out of the hospital sooner. No one in the 'prayed-for' group needed a respirator, whereas sixteen or seventeen of the others did.

The differences were so significant that if prayer had been a drug, there would have been a run on the market for it. A debunker of similar studies could find absolutely nothing wrong with this experiment and was forced to write, "Now I can truly say that physicians should take out their pads and write prescriptions for prayer." There is no way to explain these results in terms of a brain-generating consciousness in the body. The only way to understand it is that, somehow, the thoughts of one person can affect another person at a distance.

Be Creative

Once meditation becomes a part of your routine and you begin to enjoy it, you will find many more rewards. Your responses to the world around you will change. Your mind will open up to new possibilities—those that you may have dismissed in the past as being futile. You will find yourself becoming more creative in the ideas that you express. There are many examples of people who have been so influenced by meditation that it has changed their lives completely. All of them speak of a creative process that is ignited by stilling the mind and concentrating on their inner strengths.

★ Once meditation becomes a part of your routine and you begin to enjoy it, you will find many more rewards ★

Meditation transports you to another world while keeping your feet firmly planted on the ground. It is not an escape. It shows you the way to a higher level—a stage where your intellect can blossom. Many feel that it shows you the path that God set out for you.

Way 14

Think from the heart

Meditation makes you true to yourself

|Chapter Fifteen|

Expand Your Consciousness

Through meditative techniques, one can free the mind of delusions and attain what we call enlightenment.

Dalai Lama

When you meditate, your subconscious mind, which lies deep below the surface of your thoughts and influences your actions and feelings, reaches out to another in need. Unfortunately, most of us go through life without ever realising how to use this fountain of power. Only a small percentage of people discover the subconscious mind, understand it and subsequently learn how to guide its hidden powers to achieve complete success in whatever they set out to do. Meditation certainly helps with this discovery as it works in harmony with our true nature. As we experience inner peace we are led to our true self and the fact that all of us are one and were always meant to be there for each other.

When you know how to use this hidden power of your subconscious mind, you can attain riches beyond your wildest dreams. Your subconscious mind can activate your imagination and inspire you with new thoughts and fresh ideas. You can use this power to gain the financial prosperity that will offer you a new level of freedom to be whatever you want, do whatever you want and experience your heart's desire.

Your subconscious mind can help you locate your true purpose in life. It will help you determine what you are best suited to do, so you may utilise your innate talents and gifts. Through this power, you will be able to find the right position or vocation that will eventually lead you to your fulfilment.

★ As we experience inner peace we are led to our true self and the fact that all of us are one and were always meant to be there for each other ★

You can use your subconscious mind to rid yourself of frustration, anger and resentment. This guide that is already within you will help you solve your most pressing problems and lead you to make the right decision. You can also use its power to free yourself from fear, anxiety and worry. It deactivates and defuses an attitude of failure and replaces it with a more positive outlook.

Your subconscious mind is lying dormant within you, just waiting to be placed into action. Your subconscious mind is unlimited, infinite and inexhaustible. It never rests; it keeps working every moment of your life. You need only to activate it and put its marvellous power to use.

Transcend Your Inner Conflicts

When you relax, the easy feeling makes you feel good for a while and then life takes over. Again you experience mood swings, fear, anxiety and depression. You then realise that you have not yet emptied your load of regrets and grudges.

Now comes the time for the ultimate life maintenance programme. You need to form the habit of restful awareness and this is achieved through meditation.

Meditation is your way into a higher level of consciousness where you can calmly and correctly assess the various aspects of your life. Only after you have overcome and transcended your inner conflicts that have been caused out of excessive desires, ego-tripping, long-standing grudges and the need to control other people's lives, will your life become truly enjoyable. The habit of meditation is worth developing as it results in a life of joyful tranquillity. In the words of Swami Sivananda, "Meditation is an effort in the beginning. Later on it becomes habitual and gives bliss, joy and peace."

Meditation is Powerful

Here are some more facts about meditation. Meditation has been a part of all religions, since religion began. Do not meditate for the purpose of producing extraordinary powers. If they do occur, consider them merely a side effect. Withdrawing from the mainstream of life is just the opposite of what we are trying to achieve when we meditate. By bringing out our potential, meditation allows us to enjoy life to the fullest. We do not have to retreat to the caves for our sessions—the same results can be reaped even if we are to meditate in the comfort of our homes. Once the habit is developed and a routine is established, meditation becomes simple and effortless.

It is simple because it works in harmony with your true nature or your higher consciousness. The state of total health, peace and happiness is already there, all you have to do is use a technique to arrive at it. Meditation is a very powerful, efficient and safe way of doing this. It is a technique that has proven itself for thousands of years.

Find a Need and Fill it

Through meditation, the higher consciousness is given a chance to inundate your mind. We experience glimpses of our higher consciousness at various stages of our lives—moments of utter peacefulness, feelings of bliss. This is the higher consciousness expressing itself but because our minds live on the thinking level constantly, these moments are rare.

★ Meditation is your way into a higher level of consciousness where you can calmly and correctly assess the various aspects of your life ★

In fact, when your mind is crowded with thoughts, the functioning of your innate intelligence is restricted. But to be successful in any aspect of our life, we must make greater use of it. One of the principles many achievers use is: find a need and fill it. The same principle applies to your subconscious mind. You must give it a goal to reach, an objective to achieve, before it will get into action. Your subconscious mind operates best in a climate of faith and acceptance, confidently expecting that your problems will be solved, obstacles removed and goals achieved. It is the mental state that intensifies thought and causes the subconscious mind to function at its best. Though I have written about reaching this sublime state extensively in *The Little Manual of Enlightenment*, here is a six-step procedure that will help beginners activate the power of the subconscious mind:

1. Know exactly what it is that you want to accomplish. Be specific about the goal you want to reach, the objective you want to attain.

2. Believe in your heart that your subconscious mind will deliver the answer you want or need.

3. Separate fact from opinion. Do your homework and gather all available facts on the subject.

4. Feed those facts into your subconscious mind with your request for an answer.

5. Relax. Wait patiently and watch diligently for the answer to your question or the solution to your problem. In due course it will come.

6. Take immediate action when your answer arrives.

The first five steps are critically important, but unless you follow through and take action, all the preceding work will have been wasted. You will soon discover that if you fail to act, your subconscious mind will reach the conclusion that you are not serious about your requests for help.

Most scientific breakthroughs, great musical compositions, inspiring books and all other good ideas for original accomplishments, are born within the subconscious mind. The subconscious mind is the source of all inspiration, all motivation and the excitement that rushes over you by a new idea or possibility. It is the source of hunches, intuition and flashes of brilliance. Activate it with meditation and see a new person emerging. For meditation does what nothing else can—it introduces you to yourself.

★ Believe in your heart that your subconscious mind will deliver the answer you want or need ★

The joys of discovering yourself are unmatched. As you progress in this new familiarity with your own feelings, impressions and inner impulses, you will see yourself differently. You will find someone you have not known well enough before—a more spiritually aware you. You will have found yourself.

Way 15

Believe in yourself

Meditation is your path to what you really are

15 Effective Ways to Discover Your Inner Self

Way 1

Decide!

Meditation always proves to be restful and relaxing

Way 2

Sit still

Meditation gives you a positive outlook

Way 3

Relax!

Meditation expels all tension from the body

Way 4

Be strong

Meditation makes you self-reliant
and helps you attain inner strength

Way 5

Be patient

Meditation is a simple technique
that almost everyone can enjoy

Way 6

Control your breath

Meditation improves with conscious breathing

Way 7

Be focussed

Meditation helps you to take charge of your life

Way 8

Be upbeat

Meditation makes you aware of who you are

ஐ ஐ

Way 9

Open your mind

Meditation allows you to evolve constantly

Way 10

Let go

Meditation helps you to face
your worries and cope with them

Way 11

Do one thing at a time

Meditation helps you to simplify your life

Way 12

Surrender!

Meditation is the best way to overcome the ego

Way 13

Be yourself

Meditation improves your relationships

Way 14

Think from the heart

Meditation makes you true to yourself

Way 15

Believe in yourself

Meditation is your path to what you really are

About the Author

Born and brought up in a business family in India, Vikas Malkani was the head of a large business enterprise when Awakening struck him at the age of 29. He has been called many things over the years: Spiritual Guru, Zen Master, Motivator, Mystic, Rich Monk, TV celebrity, Soul Coach and Reiki Master, to name a few. Other than that he is the founder of SoulCentre and a best-selling author.

Today, Vikas is considered one of the world's leading contemporary spiritual teachers. He teaches people to be successful in all aspects of life: the physical, emotional, mental and spiritual. His forte is to make the ancient wisdom of the spiritual masters simple to understand and easy to apply to create a life of health, harmony and abundance on all levels.

Vikas is a disciple of Swami Rama of the Himalayas and has been trained in the wisdom lineage of the Himalayan Masters that involves the disciplines of meditation, spiritual wisdom

www.vikasmalkani.com
www.soulcentre.org

and yoga. A gifted orator, he is a keynote speaker at many international conferences and summits. He leads life-transforming workshops for adults and is also the creator of the SoulKids™ programme for children, which has made thousands of confident and creative children worldwide.

Vikas Malkani has been interviewed in many international newspapers and magazines and been a guest on numerous television and radio shows. His writings on self-awareness and spiritual wisdom appear regularly in magazines on yoga, holistic health and the spa industry. His television show airs on prime time every night on a national spiritual channel in India.

The Little Manual of Enlightenment

7 Valuable Tips for Those in Search of Awareness

Enlightenment is your birthright, let me show you how to arrive there, writes best-selling author Vikas Malkani in this book, *The Little Manual of Enlightenment*. These seven powerful tips take you to the world within and show you a whole new way of living. Learn how to live as a child of God, secure in the belief that the universe reflects you and your innermost thoughts. An essential guidebook for those in search of enlightenment.

Published by : Unicorn Books

The Little Manual of Happiness

7 Simple Steps to a Joyful Life

Best-selling author Vikas Malkani shares with us in this new book, *The Little Manual of Happiness*, seven steps that can lead us to having a joyful life, a life that is happy in the true sense of the word. This manual tells us to choose happiness; to live in the present; to think happy thoughts at all times and to make a special endeavour to connect with joy. A complete guide to happiness, this book will change you forever.

Published by : Unicorn Books

The Little Manual of Success

9 Essential Secrets of Self-Made Millionaires

Best-selling author Vikas Malkani shares with us in this new book, *The Little Manual of Success*, the nine secrets that will lead us to success. These include taking responsibility for your acts, believing in yourself, rejecting mediocrity, following your heart and being persistent. These are the characteristics and qualities of super-achievers. This manual tells us that we, alone, will define what success means to us. It also teaches us to create a life of our choice.

Published by : Unicorn Books

Testimonials for Vikas Malkani and His Teachings

The principles and wisdom of meditation have made my life simpler, better and more successful. It has given me the centre within myself and it makes my perception more optimistic. I find my mind becoming softer and less rigid, which also benefits my body.

Koji Kuze, Japan

Meditation has helped me to know and understand myself better and to be more in touch with my inner self. It has developed my intuition and my openness to higher wisdom. It helps me tremendously in my holistic practices. It has made me a calmer, more centred person and helps me to stay stable through difficult times.

Pamposh Dhar, holistic therapist, India

Meditation has enabled me to gain control of my inner emotions and taught me to focus those emotions to my advantage in my everyday life. It has energised me. I am more relaxed, more patient, calm and happy.

Anton Baranyay,
South Africa

Meditation has helped me move to the present and look at things more positively. I find it very calming. It has also helped me to be in a state of constant open-mindedness. I am far calmer and happier. Vikas is an excellent teacher of meditation.

Kate Harcourt-Baldwin,
South Africa

Testimonials

The benefit of meditation in my life is unquestion-able. It has taught me to be more relaxed, calmer and even-tempered.

Chris Joseph, South Africa

Meditation has helped me to become more focussed, happier and patient. I have become calmer and more reflective. In times of stress I find that I am now reacting positively to situations.

Nikhil Karur, India

I became calmer by practising meditation. My interaction with others is filled with love. I take responsibility for my life and I am happy every day of my life. I am deeply grateful that I was able to learn this from Vikas.

Mona Boehm, Austria

Meditation has helped me to have peace of mind and to control my emotions better. I have become more patient.

Eric Tan, Singapore

Meditation has given me a much clearer understanding of how we create our reality. I have changed so much; I am still trying to understand the full meaning of all the changes that I can feel taking place inside me. I enjoy life moment by moment. The lows of life do not influence me so much now. I am constantly in a state of inner peace. I rate Vikas as an excellent teacher of meditation.

Chia Eng Heng, Singapore

Testimonials

Meditation has helped me to be calmer and to take control of myself and my mind. I feel a one-ness within myself and with everything around. The training in meditation with Vikas has been very good for me.

Cassiopea Yap, holistic therapist, Singapore

By practising meditation I am beginning to have clarity of my thoughts, emotions and actions. I am beginning to understand my purpose in this life and I am able to still my mind.

Myrna McMahan, USA

Meditation is a beautiful and wonderful journey to a state of balance and calmness within you. Vikas is a living embodiment of the truth. Enlightenment is available in this moment to us all and he shows us how.

Chia Eng Heng, Principal Engineer,
Siemens Automotive, Singapore

Meditation has now become part of my life since I started practising the technique of going within myself. It was a discipline that I would not have imagined I was able to undertake three months ago as I did not see myself as the type who would be able to sit still, let alone focus the mind single-pointedly.

Testimonials

My initial practice sessions were very trying and frustrating as my physical body and mind were not keen on being focussed, just as I had thought. And I then realised that my mind and body were working overtime to make that very thought come true.

I quickly became aware of the resistance my mind and body had against my efforts to calm and focus them. Not wanting to let my mind and body win me over, I persisted with my daily morning sessions. At this point, with this awareness and personal challenge to undertake, I immediately realised that the level of resistance from my mind against my morning practices subsided; with that my body also became calmer. Subsequent sessions then became easier and more enjoyable. I was able to feel the peace and 'no worries' within me as I calmed, tamed and focussed the mind.

Meditation is now a lifelong tool I am learning and applying to all my life situations. When my mind gets tough and stresses me, I get tougher knowing that I can always find and feel the peace within me.

Lim Yuin Pin, entrepreneur, husband, father, Singapore